S0-BFE-504

Our Government

The U.S.
Senate

by Muriel L. Dubois

Consultant:
Steven S. Smith
Kate M. Gregg Professor of Social Sciences
Washington University, St. Louis, Missouri

Capstone press
Mankato, Minnesota

First Facts is published by Capstone Press,
151 Good Counsel Drive, P.O. Box 669, Mankato, Minnesota 56002.
www.capstonepress.com

Copyright © 2004 by Capstone Press. All rights reserved.
No part of this publication may be reproduced in whole or in part, or stored in a
retrieval system, or transmitted in any form or by any means, electronic, mechanical,
photocopying, recording, or otherwise, without written permission of the publisher.
For information regarding permission, write to Capstone Press,
151 Good Counsel Drive, P.O. Box 669, Dept. R, Mankato, Minnesota 56002.
Printed in the United States of America

Library of Congress Cataloging-in-Publication Data
Dubois, Muriel L.
    The U.S. Senate / by Muriel L. Dubois.
    p. cm.—(First facts. Our government)
    Summary: Introduces the United States Senate and how a bill becomes a law.
    Includes bibliographical references and index.
    ISBN-13: 978-0-7368-2290-9 (hardcover)
    ISBN-10: 0-7368-2290-9 (hardcover)
    ISBN-13: 978-0-7368-4695-0 (softcover pbk.)
    ISBN-10: 0-7368-4695-6 (softcover pbk.)
    1. United States. Congress. Senate—Juvenile literature. 2. Legislators—United
States—Juvenile literature. 3. Legislation—United States—Juvenile literature. [1.
United States. Congress. Senate. 2. Legislators. 3. Legislation. 4. United States—Politics
and government.] I. Title. II. Series.
JK1276.D83 2004
328.73'071—dc21   2002156197

Editorial Credits
Christine Peterson, editor; Jennifer Schonborn, series and book designer; Jo Miller,
    photo researcher; Eric Kudalis, product planning editor

Photo Credits
Comstock.com, cover
Corbis/Jennie Woodcock, Reflections Photolibrary, 5
Folio Inc, 9
Getty Images, 19; Alex Wong, 7; Brian Gomsak, 10–11; Tim Boyle, 17; Hulton
    Archive, 20
Photri-Microstock, 12–13, 15, 16

1 2 3 4 5 6 08 07 06 05 04 03

Table of Contents

A Law to Keep Children Safe

The U.S. Senate writes bills that become new laws for the country. In 2002, senators passed a law to keep older children safe in cars. Senators said seat belts and booster seats must fit older children better. The U.S. Senate helped keep children safe.

Constitution

Legislative Branch

Executive Branch

Judicial Branch

The U.S. Constitution tells how government works. The legislative branch passes bills that can become laws. The executive branch signs bills into law. The judicial branch explains laws.

Congress is part of the legislative branch. The
Senate and House of Representatives make up
Congress. Senators meet at the Capitol building
in Washington, D.C.

A Bill Becomes Law

Congress and the president need to agree on a bill. A bill then can become a law. The House and Senate vote on a bill. If Congress passes the bill, it goes to the president. The president signs the bill into law or vetoes it. A bill that is vetoed does not become law.

 Fun Fact:
Bills are printed with gold letters and tied with a ribbon. The are then put in boxes and sent to the president for signing

Who Can Be a Senator?

Voters in each state choose two senators. Senators must be at least 30 years old. They must be U.S. citizens for nine years or more. They must live in the state where they are elected. Senators serve for six years. They then can run for office again.

 Fun Fact:
In 1787, state governments chose the first senators. Since 1913, people in each state have voted for senators.

SENATE

11

The Number of Senators

When the United States was formed, leaders made a decision. Leaders said each state would have two senators. One hundred men and women serve in the Senate. Senators work for all people in their state.

 Fun Fact:
More than 1,870 men and women have served as U.S. senators.

A Senator's Job

The Senate and House work together. They both write bills. They both decide how to spend government money. The Senate also has different duties than the House. Only senators can vote on agreements with other countries. Senators vote on the president's choices for leaders.

Senators Keep Busy

Senators have busy days. They read new bills and letters from citizens. Senators meet with the president and other leaders. They talk about ideas for new laws.

Some days, senators visit with children to talk about the country. Senators also meet with people from their home state. Senators give many speeches. They go to important events.

The Leader of the Senate

The U.S. vice president leads the Senate. Vice presidents are called the president of the Senate. They only vote on a bill when there is a tie. The vice president sometimes is not there. The Senate then chooses another member to be the leader.

Fun Fact:
The president of the Senate uses a special gavel. The gavel is made of ivory and has no handle.

Amazing But True!

In 1814, the Senate bought 6,000 books from Thomas Jefferson. During the War of 1812 (1812–1814), British soldiers burned down the Capitol building. More than 3,000 books were lost in the fire. The Senate wanted to buy more books and start a new library. Jefferson offered to sell his books. Jefferson was president from 1801–1809. The Senate agreed to pay nearly $24,000 for the books. Today, those books are part of the Library of Congress.

Hands On: If You Were a Senator

Senators write bills that become laws. What laws would you make as a senator? Write your ideas in a letter to a U.S. Senator.

What You Need

Pencil   An adult to help
Paper   Postage stamp
Envelope

What You Do

1. Think of an idea for a new law.
2. Write a letter to a U.S. Senator. Use a pencil and paper to write a letter. Start your letter with the greeting "Dear Senator."
3. Explain your idea for a law. You may want to begin your idea with "If I were a senator, I would...."
4. Mail your idea for a law to a senator from your state. Addresses for all senators can be found at the official Senate Internet site, *http://www.senate.gov*. Ask an adult to help find your state on the list. Addresses can also be found at your local library or newspaper.
5. Put a postage stamp on the envelope.
6. Ask an adult to help you mail the letter.

Glossary

bill (BIL)—an idea for a new law

citizen (SIT–i–zuhn)—a member of a country or state who has the right to live there

elect (e-lekt)—to choose someone

executive (eg-ZEK-yoo-tiv)—the branch of government that makes sure laws are followed

judicial (joo-DISH-uhl)—the branch of government that explains laws

legislative (LEJ-uh-slay-tiv)—the branch of government that passes laws

veto (VEE-toh)—the power or right to stop a bill from becoming law

vote (VOHT)—to make a choice in an election

Read More

Fitzpatrick, Anne. *The Congress.* Let's Investigate. Mankato, Minn.: Creative Education, 2003.

Murphy, Patricia J. *The U.S. Congress.* Let's See Library, Our Nation. Minneapolis: Compass Point Books, 2002.

Internet Sites

Do you want to find out more about the U.S. Senate? Let FactHound, our fact-finding hound dog, do the research for you!

Here's how:
1) Go to *http://www.facthound.com*
2) Type in the **Book ID** number: **0736822909**
3) Click on **FETCH IT**.

FactHound will fetch Internet sites picked by our editors just for you!

Index